To A J.

Best wishes for your future.

Sam & Merle Lindsay.

SOUTH ISLAND WIDE

Photography
PETER BUSH

Moa
Beckett

Acknowledgements

The photographs in this book were supplied by:

Peter Bush

Fotopacific

Hadden Lowrey

Barbara Todd

Cover – The TSS *Earnslaw* steams across Lake Te Anau, with the Remarkables in the background.
Endpapers – West Coast waves crash at the base of the Pancake Rocks at Punakaiki, north of Greymouth.
Title page – A MacKenzie Country farmer and his dogs at work in the foothills of the Southern Alps.

ISBN 1-86958-123-7

© Moa Beckett Publishers Limited

Published in 1994 by Moa Beckett Publishers Limited
28 Poland Road, Glenfield, PO Box 100-749, North Shore Mail Centre, Auckland 1330

Printed through Bookbuilders, Hong Kong

SOUTH ISLAND

The beginning of European settlement in New Zealand and the birth of photography both happened in the 1840s. New Zealand, with its amazing sweep of scenic grandeur, seemed made for photography, and the pioneering photographers of the past century captured the emergence of a nation against magnificent scenic backdrops. Heavy, cumbersome cameras gradually gave way to the Box Brownies and eventually the "point and shoot" cameras which nearly every tourist wears these days.

To travel round New Zealand and not record the stunning beauty of mountain and forest, sea and lake, and the evocative interplay of light and shadow, is to miss one of the delights of touring this country.

From the towering peaks of the Kaikoura Ranges to Christchurch in spring; from the boom of foam-laced breakers at Waikawa Bay to a golden autumn countryside reflected in the mirror-like surface of Lake Hayes; from the wild moody beauty of the West Coast to the thrill of looking down on Lake Wakatipu from a Queenstown gondola, the spectacular landscape offers visual contrasts and experiences that are unique.

My home in Wellington overlooks Cook Strait, that restless stretch of sea often referred to as the "Strait of Adventure". On the other side of the Strait, the towering peaks of the Kaikoura Ranges seem to issue a challenge to come and visit. Each time I embark on a "Panoramic Saga of the South" with my camera I find more scenic spots which had escaped me on my previous visits.

This book is a record of all those hours I have spent enjoying and photographing the natural beauty that is New Zealand's heritage.

The *Aratika* interisland ferry steaming in to berth at Picton.

Uniform rows of grapevines march across the plains
on the outskirts of Blenheim.

A whale turns on a show for a group of whale watchers off the Kaikoura Coast.

Overleaf – Victoria Square, Christchurch.

A breathtaking view of Christchurch by night from the top of Mt Cavendish.

Punting on the Avon, with the Christchurch
Town Hall on the right.

Overleaf – Mustering sheep in the tussocky expanses
of the Mesopotamia area.

The Church of the Good Shepherd on the shores of Lake Tekapo.

Overleaf – Mt Cook village with the majestic backdrop of Mt Sefton (left) and Mt Cook (centre back).

The road snaking through the remote beauty
of Lindis Pass.

The Moeraki Boulders of North Otago nestle in the
sand like huge dinosaurs' eggs.

A distinctive Dunedin landmark – the clock tower at
Otago University.

A cascading veil of water – the Purakaunui Falls
in the Catlins District.

Sheep graze on the pastures of
Eastern Southland.

The deep, still waters of Doubtful Sound.

Overleaf – Trampers stop to enjoy the wild beauty of the MacKinnon Pass region of the Milford Track.

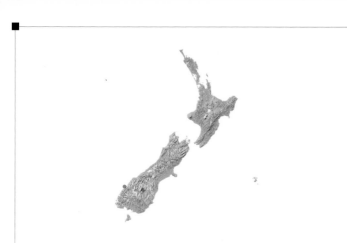

The "Lady of the Lake", TSS *Earnslaw*, steams
across Lake Wakatipu with the craggy peaks of
The Remarkables in the background.

Previous spread – Milford Sound, dominated by the
towering Mitre Peak (centre left).

Riding high on the gondola to Bob's Peak (446 metres)
with Queenstown sprawled below.

The thrill of jet boating on the Shotover River,
Queenstown.

Overleaf – The cottages of early settlers still line the
main street of Arrowtown.

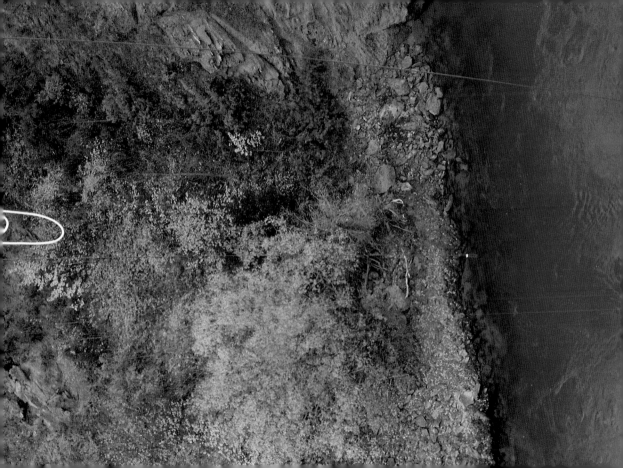

The Rippon Vineyard lines the tranquil shores of Lake Wanaka.

Previous spread – A leap of faith . . . a bungy jumper takes flight from the Kawarau River Bridge.

Sightseers fly in by helicopter to marvel at the frozen
beauty of the Franz Josef Glacier plateau.

Previous spread – The Fox Glacier cuts an icy path
through the mountains. Fotopacific

The moody beauty of the Buller Gorge with
Hawkes Crag (centre left).

Previous spread – Arthur's Pass – one of three passes across
the Southern Alps – with the Otira Gorge below.

Holidaymakers line the golden sands of
Kaiteriteri Beach.

Overleaf – After walking the Abel Tasman Park Track,
a group gathers at Totoranui Beach to board their
boat for the return journey.

Footprints leave a trail in the white sands of
Farewell Spit.

A brown kiwi searches for food – the nocturnal birds are a national symbol.